And So

Also by Joel Brouwer

Exactly What Happened

Centuries

And So

Joel Brouwer

Four Way Books
Tribeca

Editorial Office
Four Way Books
POB 535, Village Station
New York, NY 10014
www.fourwaybooks.com

Library of Congress Cataloging-in-Publication Data

Brouwer, Joel, 1968-
 And so / Joel Brouwer.
    p. cm.
 ISBN 978-1-884800-91-7 (pbk. : alk. paper)
 I. Title. PS3552.R68245A8 2009
 811'.54--dc22

                              2008043327

This book is manufactured in the United States of America and printed on acid-free paper.

Four Way Books is a not-for-profit literary press. We are grateful for the assistance we receive from individual donors, public arts agencies, and private foundations.

This publication is made possible with public funds from the National Endowment for the Arts and from the New York State Council on the Arts, a state agency.

Distributed by University Press of New England
One Court Street, Lebanon, NH 03766

[clmp]

We are a proud member of the Council of Literary Magazines and Presses.

Contents

for Mary Karr

The height of the adventure is the height
Of country where two village cultures faded
Into each other. Both of them are lost.

— Robert Frost

The new meat is eaten with the old forks.

—Bertolt Brecht

A Report to an Academy

And so among the starry refineries
and cattail ditches of New Jersey
his bus dips from egg-white sky into shadow.
When he next looks up from Kafka a blur
of green sanatorium tile flows by
then presto, Port Authority, full daylight.
He has been cheated of: the river, dawn,
a considered fingering of his long
and polished rosary of second thoughts.
Is it any wonder children are born
weeping? Out to Eighth Avenue to walk
twenty blocks home to her sleeping curve
beneath a sheet. He cracks three eggs into
a bowl and says to each, Oh *you* got trouble?
The yellow yolk is his, the orange is hers,
the third simply glistens, noncommittal.
Except to mention Kafka's restlessness
before his death, his trips from spa to spa
to country house to sanatorium,
and that she's awake now, sweet with sleep sweat,
patting her belly's taut carapace and yes
hungry as an ape but first a kiss mister
how was your trip and what have you brought us,
and that the knowledge that dooms a marriage
is the knowledge prerequisite to marriage,
the poem has nothing further to report.

The Mona Lisas

Because something there is that doesn't love
the silky mist of *nulli secundus*
surrounding famous paintings, each tourist
to the Louvre carries a camera and,
determined and devout as Pizarro
hacking through Peru, holds it high to clear
the crowd and double the Mona Lisa.
Like the johns blocks away on Rue St. Denis,
climbing narrow stairs to rendezvous
with rouged *filles de joie*, each photographer
wants to believe he's the first to touch her
quite like this, to see her from exactly
that angle, that his possession of her
is utter and unlike any other. Picture
a quilt of all these 4 x 6 trophies—
the jostled, flash-besmirched, grainy, and crisp—
a wave of smirks stretched to a horizon
where the sun, inscrutable behind bullet-proof glass,
refuses to rise. Or imagine you
are the sun, regarding the world, as each
forgotten photo in its album or shoebox
in Lima, Kyoto, San Diego,
begins, slowly, to glow, and grow brighter,
a filament resisting the amperage
of its solitude, until the earth burns
white as it moves in darkness, your smiling
dazzled double, good neighbor, fresh rival.

A Reparation

She said one fall Sunday some years ago she drove down to Pine Ridge and it sounds ugly, she's ashamed to admit it, but she went because she was so depressed, even with the pills, and she thought Pine Ridge, which she'd heard was so miserable, might put her own misery in perspective. She said she had actually been thinking that way then. As she drove, the dark knots of horses scattered across the hillsides made her want to ride and the streams of empties in the ditches made her want to drink and handmade signs said *Turn Here for Trail Trips* but she didn't have any money and party store signs said *Bud Case 16.99* but she didn't have any money. She stopped at Wounded Knee. She said to pay my respects I guess. She climbed the hill and read the chiseled names on the monument and took photos of the spray-painted sign that said *Mass grave area! No soliciting!* A paunchy Indian in overalls rode up on a huge Arabian. He said his name was Jerry and offered to take her back down the hill to her truck. Yes, he said, for free. As they picked their way down the dusty red path, he told her the dead were buried up on the ridge where the big Hotchkiss guns had lunged and recoiled, spitting a shell a second on the sleeping village below. She could tell Jerry had told this story before. Chief Bigfoot, already half-dead of pneumonia, lay in pieces in the dry snow. Blood gushed like a river from Yellow Bird's mouth. We know that on account of his son, who was only four years old at the time but all his life claimed to remember every detail of that morning. She could feel the horse's damp ribs through her jeans. Jerry's long hair smelled like soap and bacon. They came to the tin-roofed shack at the base of the hill where Jerry sold dream-catchers to tourists, of which there were never many and none but her that day. She said she wished she had some money to buy an arrowhead but Jerry didn't seem to hear her. He told her his horse had almost gotten a part in *Dances With Wolves*. That after AIM's takeover in '73 his uncle who had refused to join the protesters came home one night, flicked a light switch, and his house blew up. That he had a cousin who lived in Rapid City and worked at the Gap. He asked if she could spare five dollars. She said she didn't have any money. He asked if she could maybe buy them some beer. She said she didn't have any money. Jerry had a pack of Marlboros and together they smoked most of them before it started to get dark and she thanked him for the ride and the stories and the smokes and got into her truck and drove home. And why did she think Jerry kept asking for money after she'd told him she didn't have any? She said yes, she had wondered about that a lot. Oh, and she just remembered his horse was named Starburst, like the candy.

In Illo Tempore

The sun didn't strike the truck's roof
so much as clutch it and squeeze, crush
to cinders what little sea breeze
they had, force the last drops from their
rinds. A tanker fumbled toward them
across the greasy water. Dazed
by a lunch of oysters and beer,
the haywire hip-hop bursting like
tin confetti from the AM,
throat-thick and desperate after
months apart, they pressed together,
rubber sunk in asphalt, octopus
twisting the lid from a jarful
of fish, fingers pressed to lips, to
dust-filmed skin, down blue hollow
and cool shadowed nape, and later
on the beach he pulled like a gull
dragging a broken wing, she pushed
back like crabs clawing the pot,
and at dusk the sun turned chemical
sherbet behind the derricks blinking
along the horizon. He can
still see her, wrenching a straw purse
from wet sand—*Sunny Mazatlan*
and a grinning green parrot—and
when she turned it over tangled
seaweed, tiny blue crabs, pink and
yellow spiral shells, gush of silt

glossy black with tar, starfishes
tumbling pale and spent back to earth—
An underworld! Salty, out of
nowhere, oxygen-staggered, ours.

Synthesis and Destruction

On days the wind was stitched with ice and jays
harassed fat squirrels in the grapevines they'd drive
out past the high school track and long-defunct
Purina plant to the farm stand for squash,
bread and butter pickles in Ball jars topped
with gingham skirts, shagbark hickory nuts
in plastic bags, and musky fresh morels.
His heart spun with ease. A missile's gyroscope.
Back in the kitchen, as cats threaded their
ankles, they'd step into their stock roles sure
as filings to a magnet or spilled wine
seeping into a dishcloth: she to stove
and he to the cutting board. What did that
symbolize, synthesis and destruction?
The star onstage and prompter hissing lines
from his lair among the footlights? What are
the words, *sous* and *saucier*? They're French,
that's certain. And certain the syrah, Monk,
and parsley. Certain the dark blue napkins,
night's darkness, weak candlelight, and the half-
memorized soliloquy (how if her father
found she'd left a wooden spoon in water he
would hit her with it) he's not forgotten.

And the Ship Sails On

He faced the sink, one foot up
on the edge of the tub. She stood
behind him, reaching around.
In the mirror, her face rose
over his shoulder like the moon,
and like the moon she regarded him
beautifully but without feeling,
and he looked at her as he would
at the moon: *How beautiful!*
How distant! No smiling, no weeping,
no talking. A man and a woman
transacting their magnificent business
with the usual equanimity. The man
as a passenger walking the ship's deck
at evening and the woman as the moon
over his shoulder oiling the ocean
with light. Deep in the ship's belly
pistons churned and sailors fed
the boilers' roar with coal. On deck
just the engine's dull thrum and
a faint click as the woman sets her ring
on the cool white lip of the sink.

A Promise

A sudden clank, and the pickup shuddered down
the shoulder to a stop. A hush swallowed them.
Wind bent lilies in the ditch. Traffic blurred
past toward apple orchards, state parks, bike trails,
one last show of Indian summer before the lights
went dim and winter came to sweep the stage
with rain and clay-colored leaves. As happened
so often, they'd been cut from the production.
They crossed the spongy meadow of clover
and pasque to an Eveready plant, called for help
from the loading dock's phone, settled to wait
for a tow back to what had come to pass
for normal. The factory's neat row of spruces
seemed clipped from an architect's drawing.
The broken truck flashed its silver instance
against the traffic like a corrupted bit
in a download or one white hair plucked
from a comb. They drank beers from the cooler
and she promised they would form a troupe called
"The Onlies," and their motto would be *Like
tigers in tiger lilies!* and she laughed
so sharply two Chinese pheasants startled
from the widening field they'd just passed through.

The Weakness

She leaned back against a paper birch and
opened her pants. He knelt down and slid them
to her ankles. The bunched knot of denim
and spring wind inhibited, then didn't.
She guided him with firm calm, an author
arranging her characters' fates, and
soon the feather ran up inside her and she said
so softly and touched his slick cheek.
This meant they should return to work, peeling
wet leaves back from the cold soil in search of
the morels they knew must be near, given
the elm, old apple orchard, and the map
from last year, hand-drawn in the road atlas.
Let no one suggest they lacked directions.

•

In *Anna Karenina*, at Levin's country house,
Koznyshev asks Varenka to go mushroom hunting.
She wears a white kerchief over her black hair.
He lights a cigar and feigns nonchalance.
The others stay behind, making raspberry jam,
suspecting, and hoping, Koznyshev intends
to propose. Who could doubt the wisdom
of such a match? She is kind and pious;
he is kind and intellectual. But Levin doubts
it will work, because Varenka is too religious,
and Koznyshev too cerebral. Levin says,

They have none of the weakness necessary
for love. Meaning that they lack the baser
instincts. Of which the mushrooms are symbols.

•

Or so says the literature professor.
But isn't interpretation heresy? Even a toxin?
What can be said for certain: In the woods,
Koznyshev rehearses the arguments
for and against marriage. He stops Varenka
beside a hazel bush and kneels as if
to pick a mushroom. Her heart turns to feathers.
He asks for her guidance: *How can one tell*
the white boletus from the birch-tree type?
And as soon as those words were spoken,
both he and she understood that all
was over, and that what ought
to have been said would not be said,
and their excitement, having reached
its climax, began to subside.

•

Things are themselves, and so must be checked
against the field guide to avoid poisoning.
She emptied the paper bag of withered
penises on the countertop and weighed each

in her palm as she would a withered penis.
Twilight built up around the house like a
house. He felt distracted and sick. He brushed
the onions he'd chopped into the trash and
dropped their skins into the salad bowl.
She said this could be a symptom. His hands
weren't his. The votives and textbooks
on her dresser struck him first as symbols
and then as conflicting instructions. He thought
if he could follow them he would be fine.

A Rehearsal

At left a yellow flat of sunlight leans
against a raw brick wall. Two cats—one white,
one black—slump along the vast windowsill
as if drugged. Their little fangs glisten.

A suggestion of steeple beyond the window,
coupled with a recording of children
shouting in the imaginary square below,
conjures an older quarter. Red sofa stage right.

Coffee table strewn with breakfast's remnants.
Dish of bloody berries, greasy pages torn
from a pastry, a coffee cup set down
absently, tilted on its saucer. And

on the sofa she's reading newspapers.
The world is dramatic but not tragic.
A stagehand lifts the hem of her dress,
shakes it softly, lets it fall, and exits.

Music squeaks weakly from an old radio.
A vase of tulips sighs on a shelf.
All is in its best place under its best dust,
and in the wings his line stalls in his throat.

Hamartia Symbolized by the Stray

who cried at their tent flap. Dakota dawn.
Frost steamed in the stubble. Crazy Horse swung
his long chalk leg over a mountain, as if
he could ride it to safety. The dog stayed
and stayed. For love, they said, because it was
their habit to mistake persistence for love.
Let's review their errors so far. Crazy Horse
never claimed he could save anyone, least
of all himself. The hound loved leftover
beans and hash browns, not them. And they loved not
each other but figures of each other set
down each freezing evening in small notebooks,
his blue and hers red, while the flashlight lashed
to the tent's crown with twine swung above them,
a metronome slowing down the tempo.
And burrowing down into the sleeping bags
they'd zipped into a single downy pouch.
And the sprays of hard white stars which bit down
on the charred November sky so soon to
snow while the stray searched the packed earth beneath
the picnic table once more before sleep.
And chocolate shakes from General Custard.
Hen-of-the-woods hissing in the skillet.
Bright green cress torn dripping from icy streams.
That no one in the world knew where they were.
The valiant rust bucket they'd ridden to get there
and trusted they'd ride back out. All of these
and more but not, it would eventuate,

each other, an error which would soon initiate
their slow dissolution, foreshadowed here
by wet green wood that would not catch, ink blanched
in rain, and gray leaves snapping underfoot
like glass eyes. Blind Crazy Horse's errant
arrow made a bridge and the stray lay down and
died on it. They covered it with a jacket
and told each other at least it didn't suffer.
But the arrow groped on toward its mark.

A Courtship

She tried to take her husbandry seriously.

He liked to loiter at the orchard's edge.

She bought chemicals to kill the brambles.

He masturbated while she put up marmalade.

Dense and aglow dark gold while she.

Cinched his tiny bridle tighter.

Demanding please additional attempts.

To test her hollows and his motility meds.

Wishing for a moustache or manly accessory.

Is to hobbled courtship wholly free.

Of pleasure as why canter when you can.

Walk is to blank that face looking back.

From a snapshot soaked in gutter snowmelt.

She could already taste the fresh fruit of.

Her turn to freak on a camping trip.

His to look back and harden to salt.

In her hot hand with hips to sink.

Deeper into his script than she could direct.

After his precious gallop and jam.

When had he grown so withered and dulled.

The man who back in that kitchen had bent.

Her just so she would smell his sweet.

Bad peaches in a chipped bowl.

And said so but he would not stop.

Or soften or slacken but dug and deepened.

Bruised windfalls into bitter preserves.

Later crying over scented candles.

Made her shiver in the slanted attic.

Colder than the books he brought.

To her cluttered desk like a dish.

Of say fruit but say so overlooking.

The ride home from the hospital after.

She jerked the sloppy jockey off her.

Dropped reins slack and dragged in mud.

Handing out carrots and candy cigars.

In the hall proving only himself.

Incapable of cracking an egg after all.

Those frozen nights aglow with porn.

Workers in the orchard numbered one.

Baby in the brambles rank and cancelled.

The Exact Change

He slaughtered a six of Miller in thanks
when his supposed schizophrenia turned
out to be mere panic, fewer than half
the syllables and "easily managed with
the new medications." Chanted that mantra
when his piano teacher's voice droned on
like an undertow beneath Chopin hours
after she herself had gone home to Queens
and when stop signs seemed to say slightly more
than stop, seemed in fact to convey highly
specific messages to him and him alone
suggesting he assume certain key
responsibilities including twenty-four-hour
telephone contact with his fiancée
"to make sure nothing bad happens to her"
and the immediate emergency
closure of the Holland Tunnel . . . Oh, come
on, Doc! If this isn't schizo what is?
And after all it took so long to nose
the rental car's savage servility
through New Jersey for Thanksgiving at her
mother's that by the time he arrived he
can't possibly have been the same person
he had been when he left Brooklyn and is
that not a kind of multiple person-
ality? It took hours. And then it was
awkward. Which could describe so many things.

The gangly half-dismantled turkey splayed
on its platter. Her stepfather's lecture
on property taxes and tougher sentences.
The seven-dollar jug of Chablis which
would come up later while he held back her hair.
Every good boy deserves fudge and he tried
to be one and earn huge loamy slabs of it.
He practiced his scales on the steering wheel
as he breezed by stop sign after stop sign
toward the tunnel, stopped to search for the
exact change, then resumed rehearsal as
she, deeply soused, snored wetly beside him
smelling like something spilled on a rug. He
keyed each étude over and over as though
there would not be many more chances or
changes which I typed first by accident
but had the chance to change for which I am
thankful. But what am I doing in here.

The Missing Thing

He rose before her every morning
to walk three rainy February blocks
to the best and cheapest boulangerie.
Our secret, they said, and didn't tell friends.
Bonjour Madame, bonjour Monsieur,
une baguette s'il vous plaît, oui Monsieur,
merci Madame, merci Monsieur.
The spell had to be pronounced perfectly
to accomplish the magic. By the time
he returned, she had everything ready,
the jam pots and butter, bowls of coffee.
Her skin still lustrous with sleep as she turned
toward him. He kissed her with his coat on, she
gleaming with heat, he with cold. *I'm only*
missing one thing, she said. Indicating
the black plastic basket on the table.

We Do What We Can. We Shouldn't.

The steps, the biscuit, the glass, the powder,
the dog, the clock. To mount a production
of Beckett the month before their marriage
seemed utterly correct, but the script, like
all their scripts, was difficult. If they lost
their way they skipped to "take me for a turn,"
but they preferred everything in order, in
its last place under its last dust, and so
penciled their margins with vigor. Earth, weeping,
ocean, wedding. A June of ukases, when
H. averred the fireflies had so over-
bred they could no longer be called lovely.
(Yes, "H. averred." There's English for you.)
Rehearsals slipped from light Spanish red to
jumbo bourbons to cosmetologists
from the storefront next door pounding the walls
with scissors and conditioners. And then
slipped deeper into the evenings, like seeds
seeking water. And scratched around their seeds
to see if they'd sprouted. S. contrived
garbage bins from chicken wire, M. trained
the spots, Z. made plans for his trip to Beijing
with F. on his lap, and J. memorized his lines—
his *mene mene* lines—down by the lake,
jaundiced by lustrous, unlovely swarms.
Which are fancy ways to say their seeds
would never sprout. Which is a folksy way
to say they were trying to sell themselves

into slavery as quickly as they could,
but no one was buying. Which is simply true.
When they stepped out of character to comfort
the weepers—*It's a comedy!*—the weepers leaped
from their seats to terrify the players: *It isn't!*
What skilled attention they received as they
died of their wounds, palms aglow with guts,
in that hour the flies give way to mosquitoes.

The Other Half's Dark

The wife sleeps in lamplight, her eyes prowling
beneath their lids. Having pressed its case all
summer, the sun rests softly on houses,
joggers, the sparse brown lawns. The verdict left
unread. The husband steers the new puppy
through the cool morning. The rubbery bird
beneath the pecan tree yesterday is
gone today; the dead squirrel in the gutter
yesterday is gone today. The husband
thinks he will clip his fingernails. The wife
is up now, in the kitchen, being told
by the orange juice carton's cap that she is
not a winner. We subsist on scattered
moments of joy and faith. Between them
our choices are patience or despair.
The puppy sniffs the dry, leaf-choked gutter
like a bored sommelier. The husband
thinks of a particular afternoon
of sex, laughs easily, without desire.
The puppy startles. A silver balloon caught
in the pecan's branches catches headlights
from the avenue and flashes back half
its message—*Happy*—

Peripeteia in a Soggy Snapshot,
Featuring Lines by Ashbery and Pronoun Confusion

If Parmigianino had done it . . .
But he didn't, so let's not dwell. One thing
was for sure: They weren't sure who did. Do it.
Take it. (The picture.) Disposable cameras
had been passed around all day, so any one
of the friends and family gathered at
Two Dragons Chinese Restaurant could have
snapped the darling candid which weeks later
fluttered from their pickup's dashboard to a slushy
Rapid City gutter. They blotted. They
fanned and blow-dried. But their smiling, well-scrubbed
avatars hemorrhaged steadily, bloomed
bruises, receded like angels of history
drawn backward into fog, and soon a darkly
dithyrambic pair bellied up in shards
of vermilion and mars to stake their claim,
riding a recurring wave of arrival that
fast established them as second souls. One
thing was for sure: The JP's homily
had miscalculated their union's math
and durability if such a quick
dip could change them from eternal duo
of joy to inky banshees. One thing was
for sure: They would be obliged to return
those charming napkin rings. Their other selves
consoled that after all no one was real-
ly ever not already in some sense

simulacra, cf., e.g., Plotinus. Um,
right. Thanks a bunch. Still, the point was sadly
rampant. Deer and buffalo topiary roamed
South Dakota's office parks. The airplanes
scratching heaven were so tiny, the geese
afloat above the golf course were of course
gigantic. Red, white, and blue plastic cups
wedged in a fence formed an un-waving flag.
In brief, tons of trouble with representation,
and countless subsequent panicky theses
in fast-food drive-thru lines. *If everything*
is surface and the surface is what's there
and nothing can exist except what's there
then everything is surface?

                        Did I just
say that?

            One thing was for sure: Mt. Rushmore
was no help. Beyond the obvious, they
had more interest in their memories
of Cary Grant and Eva Marie Saint's vows
atop a soundstage replica of Lincoln's scalp
than in the disfigured mountain itself.
Still, they stuffed the telescopes with silver—
out of duty, boredom or both at once—
and found that when the faces loomed up through
the lens, they did not look like faces at
all, but rather plain ol' boulders and cliffs.
When someone told Picasso his portrait
of Stein did not look like her, he said *It will.*

30

When someone told Picasso that Stein did
not look like her portrait, he said *She will.*
The story has been told both ways. Which is
itself another story. As I've told it,
they've been on the move. They've taken a room
at the Las Vegas (N.M.) Motor Court.
Day after tomorrow they'll peer down
into that certain volume of lack
known to most as the Grand Canyon.
(That's their kind of talking, not ours.) They drop
their duffels on the worn orange shag, open
a window to the interstate, and peer
into the snapshot, surveil us, consult
the mirror no longer theirs for as much
brisk vacancy as is to be their portion.
One thing is for sure: We have come
to resemble them, but they no longer do.
She sheathes herself in silk. He sheathes himself
in latex. They commence consummation
without troubling to pull back the bedspread.
Next was Death Valley, then Hollywood here we come.
Everything is surface. Certain volume of lack.
Believe you me. They were never surer of it.

White Suit

She said one fall Sunday some years ago in Paris she was walking down rue Monsieur le Prince to an afternoon performance at the Odéon and happened to pass a Chinese camera crew filming an actor dressed in a white suit bent intently over the gauges of a giant purple motorcycle parked at the curb. When the director shouted, White Suit sprang from the bike toward a heavy wooden door, his face a blaze of fury, though whether fueled by love or hate (or neither or both) she couldn't know. When the director shouted again, all White Suit's passion fell away and he walked back to his bike for another take. Passers-by were at first confused by the commotion, but then, when they had understood, would tuck a curl behind an ear, stand straighter, put on lipstick before passing in front of the camera. One man stopped to comb his hair. As if, she said, once they were aware of their imminent promotion from mere pedestrians to archetypal feature-film Parisians, they instinctively wanted to look their best. Which is to say, unlike they really did. And then it seemed to her that the taxis and the plane trees, the cobblestones and shop windows, even the smell of roasting chestnuts, were no longer themselves but postcards of themselves, movie versions of themselves, and meanwhile White Suit was directed to arrive again and again at his destiny—where his girlfriend was a prisoner or his long-lost mother lay dying, where his nemesis was beating his best friend or a terrorist affixed a timer to a bomb—but was never allowed to cross the threshold, was made to try over and over in vain to be the thing he was but not yet well enough. And how was the play, he asked her. She stopped stirring and turned from the stove to face him. She said it was competent but dull. A stranger had propositioned her in the lobby at intermission and she had, for a moment, considered it.

In the Crazy Mountains

With a Marlboro-yellowed fingertip,
Chief Plenty Coups traces his vision
in the scrim of liquid left by the truck stop
waitress's rag. His coffeepot is bottomless,
but he's seen the end is near: plains paved,
mountains chopped for ore. The Space Invaders
machine bleats like a lost calf, or a settler gone
mad in the mountains and shoved from the wagon
with a rucksack of hardtack and blankets.
The interstate's a smear of margarine
on a wet black plate. Sleet turns to snow
against the newlyweds' windshield, their wipers
clog, their manifest destiny again
obscured. They pull off for breakfast, take seats
near the cashier's bunker of smokes and gum.
The big Indian in the Peterbilt cap
finishes his pie and lights up. The blizzard
stutters purple across a monitor,
the screen goes dark a moment, then the storm
repeats its motion. The wife orders
her usual over easy, the husband
his usual scrambled. Let no one call them
pioneers. They can stake their meager claims
to each other here as well as anywhere.

Focus

Photograph found in the road: bejeweled hand
gripping a limp dick. All parties
suffering from lack of ambition. The hills
of Tuscany won't dapple with sunlight,
and here it is nearly noon. She didn't
much want the leather jacket, the vendor didn't
really care to sell it, she hardly tried
it on, he barely praised her beauty, then
everyone wasn't hungry and went to lunch.
The rubies won't glow. The delayed train shrugs
on its siding. The penis appears at ease.
Osteria, osteria, osteria, osteria.
I knew many words but preferred to say
the same ones over and over, like
a photographer shooting four frames
of the same subject, hoping for one in focus.
This clearly among the other three.

Lions Are Interesting

Each morning in the little white cabin
by the river they woke to a raccoon
clawing under the floorboards or banging
in the wood stove. They did not discuss this.
Instead they said it was a perfect day
to pick blueberries on the hill, or that
a hike to the old glassworks sounded good.
They were beginning to speak not in meat
but in the brown paper the butcher wraps
around it. Brown paper around dirty
magazines. Like dirty magazines, they
only traced the contour of substance: silk
over skin, skin over muscle, muscle over
bone. What's under bone? Marrow? Their forks so
small and dull. As if for dolls. You can tell
dolls from animals because the latter
are made of meat. Many eat it, also.
Lions are interesting. Lions don't eat
the flesh of their kills right away, but first
lap up the blood, until the meat is blanched
nearly white. White as the little cabin
by the river they stayed in that summer.
White as the raccoon covered in ashes,
its black eyes bottomless and bright with hate.

Lesser Evils

After a morning of work in separate rooms
she said she was going to the municipal pool
and he said he would walk along the river
for a while before they met back for their lunch
of tomatoes and cheese. But in fact she went
to the lobby of the Hôtel du Panthéon
to read the *Herald Tribune* and drink a cup
of the Irish tea she liked and he to
the little church of St. Médard. A couple
old women in housedresses knelt in the first pews.
He sat in the back, with the drunks or alone.
And at lunch she said terrible, the lanes
were filled with kids from the elementary school
or terrific, I had it to myself. And he said
a barge full of oyster shells. Then quiet sex
with the curtains drawn against the chemistry
students conducting their experiments in the building
across the street. Incremental triumphs
of exactitude and necessity. In the evenings
they liked to fire champagne corks at the vast
darkened laboratory windows. Imagining the mice
startling in their cages, imagining catastrophe.
Turning back to their tumors with relief.

The Spots

Appeared to her in Sioux Falls. Lime, lemon, orange.
And immediately

vertigo rushed up like an angry dog
to a fence. She went white, fell down the well

of herself and wept.
Late at night, in the motels, when she'd fallen

asleep, I cried too. I whispered curses to the awkward stacks
of white towels. Hating anything out of balance. Hating

her, her new failure. In the mornings
my checkbook voice returned, low and soft. For an angry dog

whose yard you wish to cross.
We both hated my balance, hated her imbalance, needed each.

Sudafed, acupuncture, allergist.
Yoga, chewing gum, Zoloft, Chinese tea.

She was afraid of going blind. She constantly described
colors and shapes, as if I had gone blind.

They turned purple. They floated. They darted.
We went arm in arm, without passion, like elderly French.

Internist. Neurologist. Ophthalmologist.
Otolaryngologist. A different neurologist. Psychiatrist.

She would not allow the warm towel over her face in the MRI.
The nurses seethed. She set her jaw and vanished

into the gleaming white tube. The machine banged like hammers
on a sunken ship's hull. She listened to Bach through headphones.

The magnetism passed through her mind in waves,
like wind through the sycamores, touching

everything and changing nothing. Her courage! If courage
is what rocks have. My God, how I loved her. Badly.

The spots were like metaphors. They told us something
by showing us something else. And so for a time

we could go on believing things were what they seemed.

Coffee and Oranges

The music on TV turned gloomy. Sharks,
she said, and sure enough. A blunt snout,
jumbled cemetery of teeth, and quick black
depthless eye thrashed the screen. Coffee
and oranges made the morning acidic.
She said, the cello is the instrument
of the inevitable. White clouds
of jasmine devoured a trellis. He said,
no, the cello is an instrument of caution.
And with that they splashed overboard into
the swells and chop and chum and his lust
for control took dominion everywhere,
like a shark, like he fucked, always either
much too much or nothing at all. He said
he'd make her a deal. If she could face
the mirror a hundred mornings straight and
say out loud she wanted one and mean it
she could have a child. That wasn't bad
enough. Six days later he came in her
without a condom. And wanted to hug
and cry about it. Brought a warm washcloth.
Said she'd misunderstood. Was this
fate or warning? Punishment or praise?
She didn't even ask; she understood
he didn't understand the difference.
She idled in the Rite Aid parking lot,
adding the omen of the stiff kitten
near the dumpster to the omen of the goth girl

flashing past on her skateboard with a bright
pink bubble perched in her mouth. Called it
a draw. Tore up the script and drove home to
coffee, oranges, the cello's inevitable
caution. A hundred mornings and no telling
on which the shark will or won't dive
through her darkness on extended fins, rip
her open, churn the bitter pith and grounds
of her insides out. The music might warn her
but the shark never will. She's gone. She's here.

A Folk Tale

Once upon a time a cut carrot stretched into a curve
like a cat arching its back to symbolize a woman.
Later, a similar carrot slid smoothly in and out
of a burning bachelor. Enter desire, disguised as
a nag mashing an apple in her gums and passing wind.
She drags behind her the cart of pleasure, empty as dark
November, save for one limp carrot shining fiery orange
in a corner. Woman and bachelor passed time hunting
mushrooms but came home hungry, mud mashed in their hair, bloodied
and cut by brambles. Desire slid down an icy hill and
into a burning barn where the carrot harvest was kept.
Villagers ran for water but their buckets had turned to,
I don't know, let's say cats, brambles, or apples. The end.

Learning Something

Some tests said it wasn't her fault. Other
tests said it wasn't his. And so the fault
was mutual and boundless. The wineglasses
were broken, and so they drank from teacups.
He mail-ordered fifty pounds of flour from
a family-owned mill in Manitoba. Picturing
a confident teenage girl urging sheep
through a gate. Boys in overalls with bangs
in their eyes. A river into which he might leap
to embrace the full moon's ripe orange image.
She mail-ordered brochures from agencies
in Cambridge and Berkeley, read them by flashlight
in her living-room fortress of couch cushions
and quilts. Glossy photographs of happy
lesbians holding up astonished infants
of every hue. When he returned from drunk-
driving batards to their confused and
worried friends they fucked in her plaid cavern,
defiantly messy and stupid with drink.
Television dogs barked in the distance
and a doe lifted her head from a stream.
Other afternoons they found places to do it
on the local college campus. In a restroom
at the student union, between the Pita Pit
and Taco Stop. In the most remote stacks
of the ready reference room. Why the campus?
Were they learning something? Spring came

and lines formed outside the office where clerks
filled out the forms for graduation. Lean foreign
chemistry students with failing teeth joked
in languages they didn't recognize.
A sign in the campus post office showed
what could not be sent where. No currency
to Nigeria, software to Iran,
foodstuffs to England. He wondered whether
he could send some bread to Manitoba.
She stopped a Chinese teenager to ask
what couldn't be sent to us. The girl smiled,
spread her arms to signify ignorance,
and she was a baby angel and flew
up from a plastic basket all colicky
and glossy with tears. With these they affixed
the necessary postage to their grief.

If Sustenance Is Sin

Here Breton and Soupault wrote Les Champs Magnétiques,
said the green copper marker on rue d'something.
The street cleaner scratching water down the gutter
with his green plastic broom so resembled my grand-
father I nearly embraced him. My grandfather
the deacon, who once poured the kitten a saucer
of Gallo left over from communion. The whole
family laughed as she ran wild through the house,
leaping spastically at all our invisible
slights, grudges, and resentments, our unspoken
little white mice with pink wine eyes. The water ran
crookedly over the cobbles collecting trash
and at last fell exhausted into the sewer.
You can take a tour of those sewers. People do.
Go downtown, past the projects, under the freeway
ramp, behind the office furniture factory,
and you'll find the church of the well-intentioned who
desired to worship among the poor but later
were unnerved by the awkwardly large crowds of poor
crowding in to cop a quick sip of sacrament.
The church got the neighborhood dives I liked to drink
in after work closed down but by God I still found
a drink, and by drink I found God, at the far end
of a plywood bar, punching the flashing buttons
on a video trivia machine, breezing
through questions about the crusades and trying not
to seem defensive. Or even to seem. His skin

had the flannel smell of historic houses you
tour with your grandparents on summer vacations
because there's nothing else to do in the little
God-forsaken town and if anyone suggests
more gin rummy you'll scream. Here is the butter churn.
Here is the cornshuck mattress where pioneers churned out
progeny in hopes they would one day make nine bucks
an hour assembling shoddy office furniture
with a pneumatic drill hanging by coiled orange wires
from a ceiling so distant we might mistake it
for heaven. It's difficult to chop your fingers
off in a punch press because to make it punch you
must press a button with each hand. I learned to press
the second button with my knee, which let me go
faster and almost got me to my quota but
not quite. My next job was to put empty yellow
bottles on a belt and watch them fill with blue soap.
The apostles were filled with the holy spirit
and then could talk to anyone in his own tongue,
even, presumably, one soaked purple by wine,
or a dizzy kitten's. Yea verily my soap
would wash away the sins of every dirty dish
on earth. If sustenance is sin. The blue soap glowed
green through the yellow bottles. My dear grandfather
the street-sweeper and deacon wore a green jumpsuit
to match the broom with which he swept earth's garbage
to its just and righteous destiny. I hate the church,
but loved my grandfather, who loved the church. Breton

built a church. He's dead too. The garbage hurried down
the gutter, desperate to drown itself underground.
You can go down there too. On a tour. People do.

"Marines Help in Effort to Stop Flow of Volcano"

She lashed his boot laces to the legs of a white wooden chair,
wrapped a red silk scarf over his eyes, wedged the braided leather
crop between his teeth. The game was if he let it drop before she
came she would whip him with it. Sunday. Near the end. Trying
anything. On television, Marines dropped huge concrete blocks
from helicopters to stanch Mount Etna's lava before it
flooded the vineyards. It was spring. Most of the vines weren't in leaf
yet, their long winding tendrils naked, bright green, and she whispered
to him as she trussed him up, hoping to keep him from kicking.
She needn't have bothered. The soldiers being interviewed seemed
strangely festive, as if the mission was a game. An empty
wine bottle glared on the windowsill. The area had been
evacuated. It wasn't a question of life or death.
A farmer whose house lay in the lava's path set his table
with bread and wine as he left. *An appeasement*, he said. Some hours
later when lava filled the dooryard an olive tree shook for
a moment in fear then spit a jet of yellow sparks and burned.

A Chance

I was years out of touch with the old neighborhood,
so when he spoke I forgot the rules and looked up.
Shorter than me, wearing shoes, not bleeding. Always
my first concerns. That's another story. This one
was an Indian, abstracted and askew as
a professor in a movie. *My key is in*
my pocket. My hands don't work. I can't get into
my building. Could you please reach in there. He held up
his hands which frostbite or Agent Orange or who knows
what had twisted into callused mitts. We watched each
other, equally incredulous. We both knew
some far-gone stories, I'm sure—once two junkies tried
to sell me a snake, and once a cop shoved me hard
against a liquor-store window screaming he'd blow my
black balls off, despite the fact I'm white—but this one
was sort of off the charts. The likeliest horrors
dropped through my mind: penis, razor blades, blood, bone, hair.
Or he screams thief. Or is one, his partner ready
to snatch my bag. Or a key. An unlovely man
who can't get home without a hand. Patrol cars rolled
by like loaded dice. In Paris, my then-wife peeled
a tangerine. We were giving it one more chance.

For All We Know Delicious

The guidebooks to China on his nightstand festooned
with prayer flags of color-coded Post-its. Lime, lemon, orange.
A careful planner even for his unlikeliest fantasies,
as if each would bestow its fortune on the most organized petitioner.
Vibrator in the top drawer, fresh batteries below. She preferred
sleep. Ruin. Sudden ungovernable leaks from the body,
and the body's slow repairs. Mice in the flour bin as sweet,
white, and plump as marshmallows. Fruit over- or under-
ripe. Call without response. Aimless walks along
the ice-callused shore of the frozen lake, where ducks
caroused in the power plant's hot effluent. No, not deluded,
she insisted, but Dionysian, like the poor farmers
in Brecht's poem who throw their coats on the failing fire.
*Come in, dear wind, and be our guest, you too have neither
home nor rest.* Again he slackened inside her, again he
proffered the reasonable facsimile. The fact that her dreams
of crushing mice under her boot could make her weep proved
representations of passion were interchangeable with passion.
She wondered if it was important to him the thing be Caucasian.
She'd have preferred a color and shape more like the lights
that either appeared to flash behind her eyes in ecstasy
or for all she knew actually did. Lime, lemon, orange.
In China, poor fishermen knot rope around the cormorant's throat
so it can't swallow the big fish it catches and instead
brings them back to the boat. The bird lives on minnows. Minnows
are still fish, he said. And sufficient. For all we know delicious.

An Aubade

She said what about San Francisco? Another
second chance. There would be bridges "shrouded
in fog." Streets "pregnant and glowing" with traffic.
Dawn, she didn't know, would maybe "draw near."
He said dawn draws near everywhere. She said
a city but a city close to nature. A backyard
scattered with birds he wouldn't be able to identify
and something exotic rotting. Avocadoes.
They'd play a game on the bridge, she'd lose
control of the car, he'd kick her foot away
and mash the gas pedal to the floor until she
screamed and they'd have a name for the game
and later it would be a story for their kids if
they had any kids later. But no city is close to nature.
Her body is a white slash beneath the green sheet.
Or "a sterilized instrument." Last night's wine dregs
are both "the color of the valley as it ignites"
and in fact that color. He pulls the sheet from her
again and says he'll cut their coffins from
a wazi'hcaka even if it leaves a gray jay homeless.
The lumber's astringency. Fuck guacamole.
Deep in her knots and sap. Faster and faster. Second
nature. And now a different dawn drawing near.

Und fast ein Mädchen wars . . .

She had told him they had told her they would
dilate with a kind of dried seaweed and
it was natural and she'd frowned trying to
hide her excitement because she couldn't
understand it. Came back in a taxi
with a can of warm Sprite she insisted
was important to finish. Then slept spread
on the kitchen floor for seventeen hours.
In the morning he fucked her ass and she
fucked his ass right back. Scaring themselves with
their laughter. Twisting gobbets of lube in
place of their putative duty to anguish.
Notice also the absence of flowers,
candles, incense, Satie's wistful plinking,
all the tender utensils yet to come.
This was back when they thought of nothing but
their holes and how to fill and empty them
to greatest effect. Before her autumn
of tea and schwärmerei with the Russian
chemistry student from the labs across
the alley. Before he drove halfway to
Omaha to screw a cashier he'd met
on the internet. Before her letter
saying she couldn't remember whether
she'd named or hated it first. Before she
understood why she'd wanted so badly
to be opened so wide. When the seaweed

swayed deep in its dark currents, natural,
invisible, abiding, and in bloom.

The Fork

And this shall be divided. For her
a tine to clip the bloody twine
that bound our meat, tine to pierce
the peach to its dry pit. For me

tine to pick a white hair from my teeth,
tine to hide and keep ready. When I
vanish I will leave it in my place,
as the escapee leaves a pillow in his bunk.

The negative set of air-colored tines
I claim as my own, to wander now
like a soldier pointed backwards
and later lay me down beside myself in.

For What the Hell They Needed It For

For Crazy Horse came to Fort Robinson
to set a rumor straight and died. For he
brought white lilies to the clinic and asked
a nurse for water. For he woke from dream-
less sleep to a child pounding on the door
of the bookmobile and the sense no time
had passed. For whoever cried for water
from the stockade. For South Dakota, land
where he drove the county bookmobile and
she adopted practical methods to
set straight abstract problems. For the rumors
about how Crazy Horse died passed around
the stockade like blankets rank with pox. For
no time passing. For no time passing. For
time passing and already September
and the practical problems of the kids
crowding around the bookmobile. For pox
rising in a dreamless dark. For her still
dreamy beneath the sedative seeing
the lilies between the water pitcher
and tissues and saying aren't lilies for
a funeral. For whoever pounded
the stockade door in fear having woken
with the sense no time had passed. For lilies
rising in a dreamless dark. For the book
about Crazy Horse and the water he
drank reading it. For manual vacuum
aspiration and related methods.

For a rumor set straight. For the mother
who told him what my kids need ain't in no
damn book so what the hell they need it for.
For my lands are where my dead lie buried.
For what they did with it after. For time
passing in the century's dreamless sleep
as forts rose on the prairie like lilies.
For the last time and for the final time.
For the book about the methods he read
under water. For Crazy Horse dead by
his own hand. For a lily will crumble
beneath its strangling gilt. For Crazy Horse
murdered. For gilt obscene and abstract, but
steadfast. For Crazy Horse wore no paint or
war bonnet into battle, but covered
himself with dust and ash mixed with water.
For it came to him to do this in a dream.

In a Motel Halfway to Omaha

At dawn she said she had to go to work and he
said not until I do it to you again slut
and she said ok whatever bad man and so
he did it to her again thrilled by his amateur
stab at cruelty—like a baby animal's first
kill, he thought, and what must be the attendant sense
of infinity—while the AC unit blew icy
mildew across their bodies. She asked did he want
to know her name and he said sure. *Dawn.* Red and blue
tulips bloomed all over the wallpaper. The thought
that it was dawn and her name was Dawn came to him,
and then the thought that he was an idiot, and
then the thought that she smelled like pizza sauce, and then
the idiot thought again. He was trying hard
to hate her but didn't. Their children kept sliding
down the banister and running back up the stairs.
She said she dreamed he had a kind of stretchy black
plastic indentation on his stomach, like a
little basket, and he wouldn't show her how to
use it. Her online profile said no smokers but
she smoked. Sunlight pressing harder at the blinds now.
She shivered and he showed her how to use it.

The Pumpkin Moment

She said one fall Sunday some years ago she drove with her ex out into the country for no real reason and somewhere around twilight near a little town called Parkston they passed a field of pumpkins, pulled the truck over to the side of the road, left it running with Neil Young playing out the open windows, crossed a set of railroad tracks, and went walking among the vines in clouds of breath and cigarette smoke. The bright orange color of the pumpkins seemed incredible, almost unearthly, against the brown vines already dying back and the bleached sky threatening any moment to snow, and wandering among those pumpkins way the hell out in the middle of nowhere she had suddenly felt lifted, yes lifted was the best way to say it, lifted into another life by that utter orangeness, by the vanishing sky, by the train tracks pointing to the horizon, the shuddering pickup with its bottle of whiskey under the seat and its box of pancake mix on the dashboard, by her stupid love for her stupid man, and she had felt a twisting in her belly and she knew what it meant, and that it was certain, and perfect, and that everything was going to be certain and perfect from then on. She had thought, then, that it was that easy. That everything had happened, everything was happening, and everything was going to happen. Of course she knew better now. Now it seemed insane, embarrassing, her little epiphany in the pumpkin patch. In a word, she said, it seems amateur. But had she been wrong then, or was she wrong now? Maybe it wasn't the pumpkin moment—she had come to call it the pumpkin moment, she didn't care if that sounded dumb, that's what she called it—what if it wasn't the pumpkin moment that had abandoned her, but she who had abandoned it? She had insisted they get back in the truck and find a restaurant somewhere and eat pumpkin pie. She'd thrown up earlier and her lover was drunk and cruel and the truck's heater was broken and there was no way there was going to be a restaurant open on a Sunday night way the hell out in the middle of nowhere but she wanted pumpkin pie and there was no talking her out of it, they'd look all night if they had to, and in fact, she said, she wanted some pumpkin pie again, right now, and what did he think of that, and she was laughing, and it seemed like it had been so long since she'd laughed, and he said pumpkins had always reminded him of babies because they're warm and wet and goopy inside, but also hollow, and she said you are every single mother fucking bit the bastard he was maybe worse.

A Parley

Desperate to somehow shock her, he had staged a final scene
in a liquor store, before a gleaming curtain of vodka,
recounting in loud and expansive detail the dozens of others
he'd had in motels, rest areas, chat rooms, their own kitchen, etc.,
but even to him it all sounded as sadly predictable
as television (understandably, since he'd invented it all
with the help of television), and after she'd asked whether
he even knew what a chat room was he ended up
weepy and pleading and pathetically horny same as always.
His rented room was a couple miles from the airport. Planes chalked
the sky with purposeful angles. The morning she was to fly
away for good he sat on the stoop and wondered which held her.
A mosquito lit on his shoulder like the little devil
in cartoons and seemed about to speak, but he wasn't in
the mood to parley and slapped it to a smudge, only to itch
a minute later and find the angel had already suckled
at his other arm and built in the soft crook of his elbow she had
sometimes liked to lick a little hill of poison, a prominence
he'd never reach the top or bottom of again. He was less
some blood but set for drink. The wind lunged at a jet and missed.

Anagnorisis in the Planetarium

Spotlighted bronze plaque: Ancients believed the moon
    Blue sweater she bought him for Christmas
Wore its own light
    For her strange painting in a pizza box
Ancient error cast to cunctate recognition
    Of a large lacquer blackbird questioning a Chinese baby
Both knowing the moon is dead dust
    So why are you asking me
To give back everything given
    My own questions
Reflection of light mistaken for light
    Questions so persistent they became their answers
Face haggard ash or *O thy alabaster skin*
    She suggested he put that on a plaque
Nooses lustrous and frayed as Saturn's
    And stick it up his ass
As traffic tightened deep into New Jersey
    Distant as the Christmas tree of knowledge
They stretched to pick the fruit
    Flew apart into stars whose old light poured down
And lit up a heaven in ruins

In Minneapolis

New Year's Eve in the city Berryman
exited as a fat drunk fish and God
he may as well have been there. You, your two
and a half schizophrenic friends, and me
lined up on the sofa like a row of empty
cages at an animal shelter sunk
in 3:00 p.m. dusk deep into a cold
case of High Life we didn't even need
to refrigerate since yep, you guessed it,
the power had been shut off the week before.
Don't forget we were smoking meth then, too.
How did you know that! Which you are you? You
like *You could have seen your breath in there if*
you had been there? Or *You whose breath I had*
begun to mix with mine like March rain
raising the river or ice deliquescing
in white wine? Or is it just *you* again?
Like like like like like like like like like like.
You you you you you you you you you you.
As opposed I suppose to "is" and "we."
Anyway. Unlikely you or we is
or like to still be awake at midnight.
It can't in fact have been 9:00 when we crashed
R's parents' party, bad off, where cousins
in khaki ate ham and her dad's golf pals
said her hair sure was something. Why did we
go there? Did R need cash or to "check in"

as agreed in counseling? Did she want
to try again to show her folks she wasn't
so much a stray as a cage from which one
had escaped? You heard a lot on TV
in those sweet old days about checking in
and letting things out but not much about
what to do when those selfsame checked-in, let-
out things called collect from Eau Claire or jail
and wanted you to get dressed right now and drive
down to Western Union, yes I said now.
Hey you who said that about the meth before:
Were you checking in or letting things out?
Are you the you who sparked your love down dark
wires toward me? Is a money order
tunneling the prairie between us at
last as we speak? Are we speaking? Am I?
How thin is the ice on the river tonight?

Fish or Like Fish

He startled to see a statue of blind
justice really did loom over the courtroom. But
remained determined to scorn symbolism.
She needed a quarter to call her lover—
the docket was full, she'd be late for lunch—
and he gave her one. It was not a taunt,
acquiescence, wager, or plea. It was
a quarter. The fact that they had done this—
even this!—together and cordially,
late nights at the dining room table with
a bottle of cabernet, sharp pencils,
A Love Supreme, and an "E-Z Workbook"
from the well-reviewed—the fact that they had read
reviews!—*Don't Pay an Attorney!* series,
as if they were learning Portuguese or
origami, was not "as if" or "like"
anything, but just that, a fact, and not
to be pressed for further significance. This
was part of the agreement. They filled out
the forms. Asked lawyer friends for language.
Made stacks of books and towels. Cooked dinner
together, said "excuse me" passing
in the hallway, and even remembered
each other's mother's birthdays. As if. Not
as if. Waiting for their case to be called,
they got hungry. The bailiff pointed toward
the snack bar in the basement, which was packed
with a class trip from the school for the blind.

In illo tempore such a gift would have
caused them to turn to each other in love
and wonder. Now, no. They didn't even
look to see. She asked for fish sticks, and he
wondered if fish sticks were fish or like fish.
The children chewed their chicken fingers
with calm deliberation, staring out at what
they saw, then conveyed their limp paper plates
with startling grace to the hinged swinging mouths
of the trash cans which swallowed everything
offered saying *THANK YOU THANK YOU.*

The Library at Alexandria

After his wife kicked him out he began to date a Serbian librarian
whose apartment was a block from the zoo. From her bathtub
he could hear peacocks cry like cats stuck in trees. Sometimes
he heard the elephant. When the Caliph kicked the Romans out
of Egypt, he reasoned the library's scrolls either confirmed
the Koran and so were superfluous or crossed it and so
were heretical. And so and so. And so what? And so, legend says,
ordered them burned. And so, legend says, the flames heated
the city's baths for weeks. And so history gets written
to prove the legend is ridiculous. But soon the legend
replaces the history because the legend is more interesting.
When the water cooled he'd twist the squeaky silver tap
like a croupier at roulette, and the peacocks would squeak in reply.
When the librarian came home from work, she'd bring him tea
and sit on the fuzzy green toilet seat to keep him company
while November twilight slowly erased their faces. Something
barked, maybe a coyote. The librarian suggested the zoo
was itself a kind of library, but whether superfluous or heretical
she wasn't sure. She was certain the scrolls in Sarajevo's library
were sacred, just not to her. She trailed her pale fingers through
the tepid water and so his cock bobbed around like a cork.
She addressed it sometimes as Caesar and sometimes as stupid.

"Volunteer Firefighter Accused of Setting Fires"

See? It's natural to act against your nature,

and so permission to love you is mine.
Yes, of course I'm "acting immature."
Shall I kiss instead this fireman's poor wife?

Please, don't cry. Talk is only architecture,
Girders flame might blacken but won't eat.
Are you sick of it yet? I am for sure.

So I'll meet you in the meadow, I'll meet
You in the street, in the narrow bed
Or wide bed, on the clean or dirty sheet,

With incendiary angels overhead
And the bones of our baby below
I'll stammer you my drooping fusillade.

Ready to strike anywhere? Didn't think so.

Gravity and Grace

Returned to earth at Schiphol, he asked
to see the family windmill and the distant
cousin laughed out loud. Loaves of cloud rose
above what he supposed could be a polder.
What if they wholly obscured the sky
and closed off his escape? How many clowns
would fit in the cousin's efficient little car?
Why is it that as soon as one human
shows he needs another, the latter draws
back from him? Also, why had he come here?
Utrecht's Dom tower, the efficient little
cousin informed him, is Holland's tallest.
The nave which joined it to the church collapsed
in a storm four hundred years ago, but
lines painted on the square show where it stood.
Now he stood, with the cousin, near a fountain
choked with sparrows. In the white diagram
of the chapel's absence. *God could create*
only by hiding Himself. Otherwise
there would be nothing but Himself.
Absurdity dressed up as logic pleased him.
Sometimes a clown is simply too sleepy
to remove his makeup before bed. Lunch
was brown bread and soup. Papers reported
an identity program's discontinuation, run
dry just as he'd arrived. Not a drop remained
for him, much less his Turkish waitress.
He resolved to pour into its absence fierce

pre-dawn scratching at the dry teats of his laptop,
sheepish prayers to clouds, meze and raki,
rolls of paper scored and scraped with penciled
genealogies, searches in the dark
for his laptop's bracket key, swift occupation
of any empty space a bracket happened
to leave open, and unhealthy amounts
of poffertjes and hash. Meanwhile, the cousin
added and subtracted numbers at an
efficient little bank, met friends for sushi,
and neglected to return his calls. *Grace fills*
empty spaces, but can only enter
where there is a void to receive it. His
void took the form of lines along these lines—
One last slaphappy passenger into
the clown car squirms, while the sky in a gesso
of mist lies buried, and sparrows to the tower
flock to fill above the vacant square
with chicks their nests—which when delivered
over ham and wine and photo albums
in the cousin's efficient but surprisingly
large garden engendered some tension. The time
had come to recede and secrete himself. And so,
with assistance from Berlitz, he rose and spoke.
Cousins, IJzeren Rita, & gastarbeiders!
Allahaismarladik, tot ziens, and toodle-oo!
On my grandfather's farm in Kikalamazoo
a silo reeking of fodder juts up
beside the barn, sanctifies itself with sparrows,

and, to grant me—beni! mij!—grace, melts
into ivy and shadow. Hasten me thence, KLM—
from vacancy into gravidity,
heavy with myself and sleepy above the tulips—
for He whom we must love is ever absent.

In the Miracle Cross Garden, Prattville, Alabama

On the road from one motel already
smeared in the mind to a dim carnival
of lubricant and red light, already
a crumbling temple, toward another motel
inevitable but as yet incredible,
we fed each other spoonfuls of yogurt
abuzz with cheerful bacteria eager
to help us eat what we'd eaten, we pulled
to the shoulder every minute or so
to kiss, we lifted up our hands and swore
with Son House's crackle from the speakers,
ain't no need changin' towns, drought's ev'rywhere
we go. Late August. Flat beer, silage, pine
sap, and grit in the hot wind. Again and
again she lifted the hem of her dress
and let it fall. Perfumes thick and sweet
as an exploded dog in a ditch. She pulled
her sticky fingers through her hair and
a vulture tottered over scenting
ecstasy. The directory of roadside
oddities drew us off County 86
and down a holler to the homestead
of one W. C. Rice, whose acre of lath
and railroad tie crosses, crosses of pipe
lashed with wire, twig and bone and log crosses,
crosses of refrigerators welded
together, mantled in rust, made it seem
vast numbers had fallen, that whole nations

had burned beneath the sun's gong, and here
were scattered their powders. But merely
seem. Only an idea was buried there.
No bacteria feasted beneath our feet
on people and what they'd eaten. Live oaks
and pole barns lay veiled in the maya
of kudzu, their essences suggested
in outline. We stooped into a plywood
replica of Christ's tomb and there played out
a ritual of resurrection, culminating
with a sudden transference of authority and
grace. Already masters of our narratives
and their every potential variation,
volition, and violation. Which is
to say in love. In love despite the tricks
of light, at first dim crimson, then screaming
surge of sweet Lord have mercy if you please,
let your rain come down and give
our poor hearts ease. Some Lord or other
had heard us, and stuck us with His big syringe
of dumb luck not just once, but again
and again, over every scalded inch
of our skins. The dead dog was modified
in the vulture's guts. If a vulture enters
the temple once, the fearful priests will flee,
but if he comes again and again he
becomes a part of the ceremony.
We had shivered individually

and severally through the sad Januaries
of our respective barren Dakota
and Long Island winters and now leaned back
to laze in Dixie's sweltering echo.
Which is to say we'd switched from grave once
to cradle again and again. Which is
to say from back to front. Which is to say
it as directly as I can which is
unfortunately not very. Son House
orbited his endless spool of hiss,
a hill lay hidden behind each hill,
crosses jutted at every angle
to indicate the infinite paths to
salvation, again and again tongue and
finger and fig and oh and oh and oh
like so and so and so, they's hard times here
and ev'rywhere you go, and the times is
always harder than they ever been befo'.
We are the land's! The land was never ours!
And so the gift outright. These she solemnly swore,
then hitched her dress to squat and deliver
herself of excess atop a hummock
of dust. Combed her fingers through the halo
of her hair and stalked into the arid
imaginary cemetery to claim
her place in the liturgy. I could see
the dark emblem of her piss in the dirt,
her pale green dress among the pale green vines,
her neck sunburned gory as an animal

splayed on an altar, but my Lord, O my
Lord, what could she see in me? *YOU WILL DIE.*
One of Mr. Rice's hand-painted signs.
True, Mr. Rice, but just the once, and not
before the faithful have gone so far as
to build a nest for their cherished vulture
in the nave. Not before countless slick black
grasshoppers have sung a lonesome song so
we'll know them hard times can't last up so long.
Not before she returns from the brush with
messes of hot hairy raspberries in each
juicy fist. Mr. Rice, so bent on One death,
accidentally suggested all the others,
and so sort of did our due diligence for us.
We wouldn't know until the snapshots came back
how beautiful we'd been. How the next motel
would later loom into view unique and
stuttering as the sun, its fat blistered
belly packed with fiery babies. How each
and every next would always be before.
Not seem but be. Threading our way among
the vacant tombs, on a dry scrape of earth
that had never tasted death, we sang our song
of love. We call it *Lord, we just can't sing
no more.* We sing it again and again.

White Hair

But one other culture had yet to be
discovered, one distinct from the others

in that he knew he could not approach it
himself. It would have to come up to him.

He waited in a spruce's dark playhouse.
Nothing had happened, nothing was going

to happen, and nothing was happening.
The hours mouthed his body with their soft jaws.

He grew lonely and thirsty. He sifted
through his pockets. A crumpled playbill, half

a pack of cigarettes, some change. And then!
The poem can now report the last language

he needed, the village which would vanquish
all others: a white hair curled in his comb.

He would be its chieftain. And whole again.
And it had always been with him. Been *him*!

To the Reader

I'm sincerely grateful for your attention. I wrote this book to please you, and I hope I have. Below are notes about some of the poems. They may not be of any interest to you; I include them just in case.

The Robert Frost epigraph is taken from his poem "Directive."

The Bertolt Brecht epigraph is taken from his poem "Die neuen Zietalter" ("New Ages"), as translated by Christopher Middleton.

"And the Ship Sails On" takes its title from Federico Fellini's film of the same name.

"An Aubade." "Wazi'hcaka" is the Lakota word for the Black Hills spruce, state tree of South Dakota.

The italicized line in "For All We Know Delicious" is from Brecht's poem "Weihnachtslegende" ("Christmas Legend"), as translated by Ralph Manheim and John Willett.

"For What the Hell They Needed It For." The legend goes that Crazy Horse, asked mockingly by a white trader where his lands were, replied, "My lands are where my dead lie buried."

"Gravity and Grace" takes its title, last line, and italicized passages (except the last one) from Simone Weil's book of the same name.

"Hamartia Symbolized by the Stray" makes reference to the Crazy Horse Memorial in South Dakota. Sculptor Korczak Ziolkowski and the Lakota Chief Henry Standing Bear started the Memorial in 1948; the work continues.

"In the Crazy Mountains." Chief Plenty Coups (1848?-1932) was a Crow chief who pursued a policy of cooperation with white settlers. He made frequent vision quests in the Crazy Mountains of south-central Montana. As a child, he had a vision in which the buffalo of the Great Plains were transformed into cattle.

"In Minneapolis" refers to the poet John Berryman, who committed suicide by jumping from the Washington Avenue Bridge in Minneapolis in January, 1972.

"In the Miracle Cross Garden, Prattville, Alabama" is for my wife, Wendy. The poem references Son House's song "Dry Spell Blues" and Franz Kafka's parable "Leopards in the Temple."

"Learning Something" uses several images from Li Po's poem "High in the Mountains, I Fail to Find the Wise Man," as translated by David Young.

"'Marines Help in Effort to Stop Flow of Volcano'" takes its title from a headline in *The New York Times*, April 25, 1992.

"Peripeteia in a Soggy Snapshot, Featuring Lines by Ashbery and Pronoun Confusion" uses a number of lines from John Ashbery's poem "Self-Portrait in a Convex Mirror."

"A Report to an Academy" takes its ape from Franz Kafka's story of the same name.

"*Und fast ein Mädchen wars . . .*" takes its title from the first line of the second of Rainer Maria Rilke's *Sonnets to Orpheus*. The phrase translates roughly as "and almost a girl it was."

"'Volunteer Firefighter Accused of Setting Fires'" takes its title from a headline in *The New York Times*, November 28, 1999.

"We Do What We Can. We Shouldn't" takes its title and some of its language from Samuel Beckett's play *Endgame*, a production of which is being rehearsed in the poem. The poem's last line is adapted from lines XXVI.28-31 of Dante's *Inferno*, as translated by Robert Pinsky.

"The Weakness" quotes directly and indirectly from the Maude translation of Tolstoy's *Anna Karenina*.

Again, my thanks.

JB

Acknowledgments

Some of these poems first appeared in *Alaska Quarterly Review,*
Chelsea, Crab Orchard Review, The Eleventh Muse, Gettysburg Review,
Gulf Coast, New England Review, Paris Review, Ploughshares, Poetry,
POOL, Post Road, and *Western Humanities Review.* "Hamartia
Symbolized by the Stray" first appeared in *Legitimate Dangers:*
American Poets of the New Century (Sarabande Books, 2006). My
thanks to the editors of these publications.

I would also like to thank the Mrs. Giles Whiting Foundation,
the Poetry Foundation, the Fine Arts Work Center in Provincetown,
and the Research Advisory Council of the University of Alabama
for their support.

Joel Brouwer was born in Grand Rapids, Michigan, in 1968. He has published two previous collections of poems, *Exactly What Happened* and *Centuries*. He teaches at the University of Alabama.